The Practice
of the
Presence
of God

In Modern English

Brother Lawrence

Translated into Modern English by Marshall Davis

Cover design by Ryan Rusnak

ISBN-13: 978-1-5212997-5-3 (paperback)

ISBN-10:0989835065 (ebook)

ISBN-13:978-0-9898350-6-0 (ebook)

CONTENTS

PREFACE

Brother Lawrence was born Nicolas Herman in 1611 in the town of Hériménil in the French Lorraine. Born into a poor family, he received little formal education as a child. As a young man, he joined the army and fought in the Thirty Years' War. At the age of eighteen, while in military service, Herman had an experience of God that began his spiritual journey.

During winter, Herman saw a barren tree, stripped of leaves and fruit. While contemplating the upcoming springtime and the transformation that would happen to the tree, a transformation of his soul occurred. His friend and biographer described it in these words: "At that moment he saw clearly the Providence and Power of God." Brother Lawrence had awakened to the Presence of God. That awareness of Divine Presence continued unabated for the rest of his life.

A short time after this experience (which is usually referred to as his conversion), a serious injury to his sciatic nerve forced him to retire from the army. This injury left him lame and in considerable pain for the rest of his life. After leaving the army, he lived for a period of time in solitude. It seems that during this period of time he integrated his new spiritual awareness into his life. Eventually, out of financial necessity, he took a job as footman. But within six years he had entered the Discalced Carmelite monastery in Paris. He took the name Lawrence of the Resurrection.

Nicolas entered the priory as a lay brother, not having the education necessary to become a priest. He spent the rest of his life within the walls of this large monastic community, working in the kitchen for most of his life and later as a cobbler. While assigned to the kitchen, working at the tedious tasks of cooking and cleaning, he developed the practice of living always in conscious awareness of God.

Despite his humble position in the community, his reputation attracted many visitors from the outside who sought spiritual guidance from him. The practical wisdom that he shared would later become the basis for this book, The Practice of the Presence of God. His death in 1691 occurred in relative obscurity, but his teachings continued to live on in his words.

Monsignor Joseph de Beaufort, vicar general to the archbishop of Paris, had become Lawrence's friend. He compiled notes of his conversations with Lawrence, letters written by him, and his Spiritual Maxims, which were found in his room after his death. He published these together in a single volume in 1693, two years after Brother Lawrence's death.

The little book quickly became a devotional classic among both Catholics and Protestants. In later editions the Maxims came to be omitted from English versions. No English translation of The Practice of the Presence included the Maxims after one printed in Edinburgh in 1741. Here in this Modern English edition the Maxims are reunited with the Conversations and Letters into a single volume.

The first English translation of the complete work appeared in 1724 and became widely read by English speaking readers. Among its greatest admirers was John Wesley, the founder of Methodism. Today The Practice of the Presence of God is recognized as a work of great spiritual depth by a broad range of traditions, from evangelical Christians to adherents of non-Christian spiritual traditions.

Today the book is found most often in the form of an anonymous English translation from the early 19th century. That is the edition found in Christian Classics Ethereal Library, Project

Gutenberg, and the vast majority of printed editions. This present translation is based on that early English version and another nineteenth century translation of the Maxims. This Modern English edition is complete and unabridged. It seeks to preserve the historical integrity of the original, while making it accessible to the modern reader.

The translation process has been a labor of love for this editor. I have personally found Brother Lawrence's words to be an inspiration throughout my life. I have read this short work countless times over several decades. Yet when I have recommended it to others, the response I often received was that it was difficult to understand. The archaic wording and obsolete vocabulary made it inaccessible to many who would otherwise benefit from it. With such readers in mind, I have slowly and prayerfully rendered it into language easier to understand. I pray that God may use this translation as an instrument of blessing to others.

Marshall Davis

October, 2013

CONVERSATIONS

FIRST CONVERSATION

I first met Brother Lawrence on August 3, 1666. He told me that God had done a supreme work of grace in his life through his conversion at the age of eighteen. It happened in winter. He had noticed a tree stripped of its leaves. He realized that in a little while the leaves would return, and the flowers and fruit would appear. At that moment he clearly saw the Providence and Power of God. That awareness of God had never dimmed. This experience had perfectly set him free from this world. It ignited in him a love for God that was so great that he could not tell whether it had increased during the forty years since that day.

Prior to being a monk, Lawrence had been a footman in service to Monsieur Fieubert, who was a treasurer. Lawrence described himself as a big awkward fellow who broke everything. When he originally entered the monastery, he thought that he would be made to suffer for his awkwardness and faults. In this way he hoped to offer his life and all its pleasures as a sacrifice to God. But God had disappointed him. He had found nothing but contentment in the monastery.

He said that we should establish ourselves in a sense of God's Presence by continually communing with Him. It is shameful to abandon this divine communion to occupy our minds with trivial matters. We should feed and nourish our souls with high thoughts of God, which yield us great joy in devotion to Him.

We ought to awaken faith. It is regrettable that we have so little faith. Instead of living in faith daily, people amuse themselves with religious devotions, which are continually changing. The way of faith is the spirit of the Church, and it alone is sufficient to bring us to a high degree of perfection.

We ought to give ourselves to God in both mundane and spiritual matters. We should seek our satisfaction only in fulfilling His will, whether that leads to suffering or comfort. All things are equal to a soul truly surrendered to God. There needs to be faithfulness in the dry seasons of the spiritual life, when we feel distant from God and find prayer burdensome. At such times, God is testing our love for Him. Those are the times when we should surrender ourselves to God. If we do this, it will result in spiritual advancement.

He was not surprised to hear about all the sufferings and sins in the world. On the contrary, he was surprised there were not more, considering the malice sinners were capable of. He prayed for them, but he knew that God could change things whenever he wanted. Therefore after praying, he gave it no further thought.

To arrive at such surrender to God, we should pay attention to the human passions that mingle with the spiritual desires within us. God gives insight concerning those passions to those who truly desire to serve Him. He said that if it were my intent to sincerely serve God, I could visit him as often as I wanted, without fear of being a bother to him. But if this was not my intention, I should not come to see him again.

SECOND CONVERSATION

Lawrence said that he had always been governed by love without thought of self. He resolved to make the love of God the goal of all his actions. He had become satisfied that this method was the best path. He was pleased when he could pick up a straw from the ground for the love of God, seeking only Him and nothing else, not even His gifts.

For a long time he was troubled by the thought that he would be damned. No one in the world could have persuaded him otherwise. But then he reasoned within himself in this manner: "I did not enter into the religious life for any reason except the love of God, and I have endeavored to live only for Him. Therefore whatever becomes of me after death, whether I am lost or saved, I will always continue to act purely for the love of God. I shall have this consolation at least; that till death I shall have done all that is in me to love Him."

This troubled state of mind lasted four years, during which he suffered greatly. But since that time he has lived his life in perfect liberty and continual joy. He placed his sins between him and God, as it were, telling God that he did not deserve His kindnesses. But God still continued to bestow them upon him in abundance.

In order to form a habit of communing with God continually and committing everything we do to Him, we must at first make a special effort. After a while we find that His love inwardly inspires us to do all things for Him effortlessly.

He expected that after all the pleasant days that God had given him, that he would have his share of pain and suffering. He was not concerned about it. He knew very well that he could do nothing by himself, and God would not fail to give him the strength to bear them.

When an occasion arose to exercise some virtue, he committed himself to God, saying, "Lord, I cannot do this unless You enable me." Then he received more than sufficient strength.

When he failed in his duty, he simply confessed his fault to God, saying, "I shall never do otherwise if You leave me to myself; You must stop my falling, and fix what is amiss in me." Having prayed in this manner, he gave it no further thought.

He said that we ought to relate to God in the greatest simplicity, speaking to Him frankly and plainly, and imploring His assistance in our affairs as they happen. In his experience, God never failed to grant help.

Recently he had been sent into Burgundy to buy a quantity of wine for the monastery. This was a very unwelcome task for him, because he had no head for business. Furthermore he was lame, and he could not move around the boat except by rolling himself over the casks. However he did not bother himself about it, nor about the purchase of the wine. He said to God that it was His business he was on, and then he found that he did the job very well. He had been sent into Auvergne last year on the same business, and it also seemed to work out well.

The same was true of his work in the kitchen (to which he had a natural aversion). He proceeded to do everything there for the love of God, praying continually for God's grace to do his work well. In this manner he had found everything easy during the fifteen years that he had been employed there.

He was very pleased with the position he was now in. But he was as ready to leave this job, if it came to that. He always enjoyed himself no matter what he was doing because he did everything, even the smallest things, for the love of God.

The set times of prayer were no different for him than other times. He secluded himself to pray, according to the directions of his Superior. But he did not need such solitude, nor did he ask for it. Even the busiest work did not distract him from his communion with God.

He knew that he had an obligation to love God in all things, and he endeavored to do so. Therefore he felt like he had no need of a spiritual director to advise him, but he very much needed a confessor to absolve him. He was very aware of his faults, but he was not discouraged by them. He confessed them to God, but did not plead with Him to excuse them. When he had finished confession, he gently resumed his normal practice of love and adoration.

When he was troubled, he consulted no one. He knew by the light of faith that God was present, and he contented himself with directing all his actions to Him. He did everything with the intent to please God, and did not worry about consequences.

"Useless thoughts spoil everything," he said. All trouble began there. We ought to let go of such thoughts as soon as we are aware of them. They are worthless to either life or salvation. We should return quickly to our communion with God.

At the beginning he had often used his appointed time of prayer by rejecting wandering thoughts and falling back into them. But he could never regulate his devotional life by using spiritual disciplines the way some people do. He would start off by meditating for a while, and then set it aside and resume his natural relationship with God in a manner that he could not describe.

He said that all bodily spiritual disciplines and exercises are useless. All that is needed to bring us to union with God is love. He had pondered this subject much, and concluded that the shortest way to God was to go straight to Him by a continual exercise of love and doing everything for His sake.

It is important to discern the difference between acts of the understanding and those of the will. Understanding with the mind is of little value. The intent of the heart is all important. We should concern ourselves only with loving and delighting ourselves in God.

All kinds of spiritual disciplines, if they are void of the love of God, cannot remove a single sin from our lives. We should, without anxiety, accept that all our sins have been forgiven by the blood of Jesus Christ. From this perspective we are free to seek only to love Him with all our hearts. We can take comfort in the fact that God seems to grant the greatest grace to the greatest sinners as signs of His great mercy.

He said that the greatest pains or pleasures of this world are not to be compared with what he had experienced of both kinds in the spiritual life. He worried about nothing and feared nothing. His only desire is not to offend God.

He did not beat himself up when he sinned. He said, "When I fail in my duty to God, I immediately acknowledge it, saying, 'All I do is sin, and I shall never do otherwise if I am left to myself.' If I do something well, I give God thanks and acknowledge that everything good that I do comes from Him."

THIRD CONVERSATION

Lawrence told me that the foundation of his spiritual life was a high concept and reverence of God in faith. Once he had become established in this lofty conception of God, he had no other plan except to faithfully reject every other thought, in order that he might do all things for the love of God. Sometimes when he realized that he had not thought of God for a while, he did not worry himself about it. After acknowledging his wretchedness to God, he returned to Him with even greater trust in Him, prompted by the fact that he felt so wretched to have forgotten Him.

The trust we put in God honors Him greatly and draws down great blessings.

He said it was impossible that God would deceive. He also said that God would not allow a soul, which is perfectly surrendered to Him and committed to endure everything for His sake, to suffer long.

He had often experienced the guidance of Divine Grace on many occasions. Based on that experience, whenever he had business to do, he did not think about it beforehand. When it was time to do something, he looked to God. He could see clearly, as if he was looking into a perfect mirror, exactly what God wanted him to do. Most recently he did this naturally, without even thinking about it, but previously he had used the technique more intentionally in his tasks.

When outward busyness diverted him a little from the awareness of God, a fresh remembrance would come from God and consume his soul. This presence of God so inflamed and transported him that it was difficult for him to contain himself.

He said he was more united to God in his outward work, than when he left it for devotion in seclusion.

He expected sometime in the future to experience some great pain of body or mind. The worst that could happen to him was to lose that sense of the presence of God, which he had enjoyed so long. But the goodness of God assured him He would not forsake him completely, and that He would give him strength to bear whatever evil He permitted to happen to him. Therefore he feared nothing, and he had no reason to consult anybody about his state. When he had attempted to talk to someone about it, he had always come away more perplexed. Because he was always ready to lay down his life for the love of God, he had no fear of danger.

He said that perfect surrender to God was a sure way to heaven, and in this surrender we always had sufficient light for our conduct.

In the beginning of the spiritual life, we ought to be faithful in doing our duty and denying ourselves. After that, unspeakable pleasures followed. In difficulties we only need to turn to Jesus Christ and beg His grace, and then everything became easy.

Many people do not advance in the Christian life, because they get stuck in penances and particular spiritual exercises. They neglect the love of God, which is the goal. This could be seen plainly by their works, and was the reason why we see so little solid virtue.

The spiritual life is neither an art nor a science. To arrive at union with God all one needs is a heart resolutely determined to apply itself to nothing but Him, do nothing but for His sake, and to love Him only.

FOURTH CONVERSATION

Lawrence conversed with me frequently, and with great openness, about the heart and his manner of going to God. Some of this has already been described previously.

He told me that it all consists in one hearty renunciation of everything that does not lead to God. In this manner we develop the practice of continual communion with Him in freedom and simplicity. We just need to recognize God as intimately present with us and address ourselves to Him every moment. When in doubt, we can ask His assistance in knowing His will. We can also ask his help in performing those things which we know He requires of us. We should offer everything to Him before we do it and give Him thanks after we have finished.

Part of this communion with God is praising, adoring, and loving him incessantly for His infinite goodness and perfection.

Without being discouraged by our sins, we should pray for His grace with perfect confidence, relying upon the infinite merits of our Lord. God never fails to offer us His grace for every occasion. He distinctly perceived this in his own life, and it never failed, except when his thoughts wandered from a sense of God's Presence, or he forgot to ask His assistance.

God always gives us light in the midst of our doubts when we have no other purpose but to please Him.

Our sanctification does not depend upon changing what we do, but in doing for God's sake what we normally do for our own sake. It is sad to see how many people mistake the means for the end, addicting themselves to religious works, which they perform very imperfectly because of their human or selfish motives.

The most excellent method he had found of going to God was to do our normal activities without any view of pleasing men, and (as far as we are able) purely for the love of God.

It was a great delusion to think that times of prayer ought to be different than other times. It is just as important to adhere to God by action in the time of action, as by prayer in time of prayer.

His prayer was nothing other than a sense of the presence of God. His soul was at such times unconscious of everything but Divine love. When the appointed times of prayer were over, he found it to be no different. He still continued with God, praising and blessing Him with all his strength. In this way he lived his life in continual joy. Yet he hoped that God might give him something to suffer when he had grown stronger.

We ought to heartily put our whole trust in God once and for all, and make a total surrender of ourselves to Him, secure in the faith that He would not deceive us.

We should not become weary of doing little things for the love of God. God regards not the greatness of the work, but the love with which the work is done. We should not be surprised if in the beginning we often fail in our endeavors. In the end we will develop a habit, which will naturally produce acts through us without effort, to our exceeding great delight.

The whole substance of religion is faith, hope, and love. By the practice of these we become united to the will of God. Everything else is unimportant and should be used as a means to our end, which is to be swallowed up by faith and love.

All things are possible to him who believes. They are less difficult to him who hopes. They are easier to him who loves. And they are easiest to him who perseveres in the practice of all three virtues.

The goal of the spiritual life is to become the most perfect worshippers of God that we can possibly be, in this life and throughout all eternity.

When we begin the spiritual life we should thoroughly examine what we are. We find ourselves to be miserable. We do not deserve the name of Christians. We are subject to all kinds of suffering. Our circumstances trouble us and cause continuous changes in our health, our emotions, and our mental and physical dispositions. God humbles us through this suffering and pain, inside and outside. It should not surprise us that people cause us troubles, temptations, oppositions and difficulties. We should accept these and bear them for as long as

God wishes, and view them as highly beneficial to our spiritual development.

The greater perfection a soul aspires for, the more dependent it is upon Divine grace.

Lawrence was questioned by someone in his own order (to whom he was obliged to open himself) how he had attained such a constant sense of God. He told him that since first coming to the monastery, he had considered God as the end of all his thoughts and desires. God was the target to which everything should point, and the goal in which everything will be fulfilled.

In the beginning of his novitiate he spent the hours appointed for private prayer in thinking of God. The purpose of this was to convince his mind, and deeply impress upon his heart, the reality of Divine existence. He surrendered himself to an attitude of faithful devotion and insight rather than reasoning and thinking. By this simple and sure method, he practiced the knowledge and love of God, resolving to use every effort to live in a continual sense of His Presence, and if possible, never to forget Him.

When he had prayerfully filled his mind with an attitude of great devotion of that infinite Being, he went to his work in the monastery kitchen as a cook. He considered what the job required, and when and how each thing was to be done. Then he spent all his time at work, as well before and after his work, in prayer.

When he started work, he said to God, with a complete trust in Him, "O my God, You are with me, and I must now, in obedience to Your commands, apply my mind to these outward things. I beseech You to grant me the grace to continue in Your Presence. To this end I ask that you grant me Your assistance, receive all my works, and possess all my emotions." As he proceeded in his work, he continued in intimate conversation with his Maker, imploring His grace, and offering to Him all his actions.

When he had finished, he examined himself to determine how he had discharged his duty. If he had done well, he gave thanks to God. If not, he asked for forgiveness. Then without being discouraged, he set his mind right again, and continued his practice of the presence of God, as if he had never deviated from it. He said, "By getting up after every fall, and by frequently renewing my faith and love, I have arrived at a state of mind where it is more difficult for me NOT to think of God as it was at the beginning to think of Him."

Brother Lawrence had found such a blessing in walking in the presence of God, that it was natural for him to share his practice earnestly with others. But his example was a stronger inducement than any argument he could voice. Even his countenance was edifying. There was such a sweet and calm spirit about him, that it could not but affect those who met him. It was observed that even in the midst of the greatest bustle of kitchen work, he preserved his composure and heavenly-mindedness. He was never hurried or loitering. He did everything in its season with an even uninterrupted composure and tranquility of spirit. "The time of work," he said, "is not different for me than the time of prayer. In the noise and clatter of my kitchen, while several people are calling out at the same time for different things, I possess God in as great tranquility as if I were upon my knees at the Blessed Sacrament."

LETTERS

You have expressed a sincere desire that I share with you the method by which I arrived at the continual sense of God's Presence, which our Lord in His mercy has granted to me. It is with great reluctance that I agree to your insistent request. I will do so only on one condition: that you show my letter to no one. If I thought that you would let it be seen, then all my desire for your advancement would not be enough to get me to do it.

This is how it came about. I read many books containing different methods of going to God and various practices of the spiritual life. These only served to confuse me, rather than facilitate what I sought, which was simply to become wholly God's.

So I resolved to give all for the All. First I gave myself completely to God and made restitution for my sins, as much as I could. Then out of love for Him, I renounced everything that was not God. I began to live as if there were no one else in the world but God and me. Sometimes I

29

imagined myself as a poor criminal at the feet of the Divine Judge. At other times I would behold Him in my heart as my Divine Father.

I worshipped Him as often as I could, keeping my mind in His holy Presence. Whenever I noticed that my mind had wandered, I brought it back to Him. I found this very difficult, and yet I continued in the practice, without feeling guilty when my mind wandered involuntarily. I made this my constant exercise all day long, whether it was the appointed time of prayer or not. At all times - every minute of every hour, even at the busiest time of my work - I drove from my mind everything that was capable of interrupting my thought of God.

This has been my spiritual practice ever since I entered into this religious community. Even though I have done this practice very imperfectly, I have found it to be very helpful. All benefits from this practice I attribute wholly to the mercy and goodness of God, because we can do nothing without Him. This is certainly true of me more than anyone. When we are faithful to keep ourselves in His holy Presence, and set Him always before us, this prevents us from willfully offending and displeasing Him. It also produces within us a holy freedom and (if I may speak so boldly) an intimacy with God, so that we are able to ask, and successfully receive by his grace, anything that we need.

In conclusion, by repeating this practice often it becomes second nature, and the presence of God becomes our normal state of mind. Join me in thanking God for His great goodness towards me, which I can never fully appreciate, and for the many kindnesses that He has granted to such a miserable sinner as I. May all things praise Him. Amen.

SECOND LETTER

I have not found my way of spiritual life in books. I have no problem with that, yet it would be a confirmation for me if you would let me know your thoughts about it.

I had a conversation recently with a person known for his piety. He told me that the spiritual life was a life of grace. He said it begins with servile fear, is increased by hope of eternal life, and is consummated by pure love. He said that each of these states had different stages, through which one arrives finally at that blessed consummation.

I have not followed such spiritual approaches. On the contrary, I have instinctively avoided them because I found that they discouraged me. This was why, when I took religious orders, I resolved simply to give myself to God alone and to renounce everything but the love of Him. I considered this to be the best way I could address my sins.

For the first few years, I usually used the time set aside for devotion in contemplating death, judgment, hell, heaven, and my sins. The rest of the day I would apply my mind carefully to the presence of God, even when I was in the midst of my work. I considered God to be always with me and often in me.

Eventually I naturally came to do the same method during my set time of prayer. This caused me great delight and consolation. This practice produced in me such a great reverence for God that faith alone was able to satisfy me.

This was how I began the spiritual life. Yet I must tell you, that for the first ten years I suffered greatly from the fear that I was not devoted to God enough, even though I desired to be. My past sins were always in my mind. I saw these as the reason and source of my sufferings, in spite of the great unmerited blessing of God's presence that I also knew.

During this time I would often fall and immediately rise up again. It seemed to me that all of creation, reason, and even God Himself were against me. Only faith was for me. Sometimes I was troubled with the idea that to believe I had received the blessing of the presence of God was arrogance. Who was I to pretend to be instantly at the place where others arrived only with difficulty? At other times I thought it might all be a delusion, and that there was no salvation for me.

I thought that I would spend the rest of my days in suffering. This did not diminish my trust in God, but only increased my faith. Then suddenly I found myself changed. My soul, which until this time had been troubled, felt a profound inward peace. It was as if my soul had found its center and place of rest.

Ever since that time I have walked with God simply, in faith, humility and love. I try diligently to do nothing and think nothing which may displease Him. I trust that when I have done everything I can, He will do with me whatever He pleases.

I cannot describe what happens within me now. There is no suffering or difficulty because I have no will but God's will. I attempt to accomplish God's will in all things. I am so surrendered to God that I would not pick up a straw from the ground against His will, or from any other motive but love of Him.

I have stopped practicing all forms of devotion and set prayers, except those which I am obliged to participate in. I make it my practice only to persevere in His holy presence. I do this simply by paying attention to, and directing my affection to, God. I call this the actual presence of God. It is a habitual, silent, and secret communion of the soul with God. This often causes such joys and raptures inwardly, and sometimes also outwardly, that I am forced to make an effort to moderate them to prevent their appearance to others.

In short, I am certain beyond all doubt that my soul has been with God above during the last thirty years. I have omitted many things in this account, so that it will not be tedious to you. Yet I think it is right to tell you how I approach God, whom I behold as my King.

I consider myself the most wretched of men, full of wounds and uncleanness. I have committed all sorts of crimes against my Sovereign. Prompted by heartfelt repentance, I confess all my wickedness to Him. I ask His forgiveness and give myself fully into His hands. He may do whatever He wants with me. But my Lord, who is full of mercy and goodness, does not punish me. Instead he embraces me in love, seats me at His table, and serves me with His own hands. He hands me the key to His treasure trove. He converses with me and shows his delight in me incessantly in thousands of ways. He treats me in all respects as His favorite son. This is how I come into God's holy presence.

Most often my method is a simple attention to God combined with a general sense of hunger for God. I find myself often attached to God with the great sweetness and delight of an infant at the mother's breast. I hesitate to use the expression, but the inexpressible sweetness which I taste and experience there is as if I were at the bosom of God at all times. Sometimes my thoughts wander away from God by necessity or infirmity. But soon an inner desire brings me back to God. This inward yearning is so delightful and delicious that I am ashamed to describe it.

I desire that Your Reverence reflect upon my great wretchedness, of which you are well aware, rather than upon the great blessings which God bestows on me, of which I am unworthy and ungrateful.

My set hours of prayer are only a continuation of the same exercise I have been describing. Sometimes I consider myself as a stone before a sculptor, who is making a statue. I present myself to God, and I desire Him to make His perfect image in my soul, and make me entirely like Himself.

At other times during prayer, I feel all my spirit and all my soul lifted up without any intent or effort on my part. My soul feels as if it were suspended and firmly fixed in God, as in its center and place of rest.

I know that some people say that this state is inactivity, delusion, and self-love. I confess that it is inactivity, but it is a holy inactivity. It would also be happy self-love, if the soul in that state were capable of self-love. But in actuality when the soul is in this prayerful repose, it cannot be disturbed by such former states. They would hinder communion with God rather than assist it.

I cannot bear to hear this called delusion. The soul which enjoys God desires nothing but Him. If what is within me is delusion, then let God fix it. Let Him do what He pleases with me. I desire only Him, and to be wholly devoted to Him.

I would appreciate it, though, if you would oblige me by sending me your opinion. I always take your opinions very seriously, and have great esteem for Your Reverence. I am yours in our Lord.

THIRD LETTER

We have a God who is infinitely gracious and knows all our wants. I always thought that He would bring you to the edge. He will come in His own time, and when you least expect it. Hope in Him now more than ever. Thank Him with me for the blessings He gives you, particularly for the fortitude and patience which He gives you in your afflictions. This is a plain mark of the care He takes of you. Comfort yourself in Him, and give thanks for everything.

I also admire the fortitude and bravery of our mutual friend. [His name is omitted.] God has given him a good disposition and a good attitude. But there remains in him a little of the world and a great deal of youth. I hope the affliction which God has sent him will prove to be a good remedy for this, and cause him to look inside himself. This accident will hopefully prompt him to put all his trust in the One who accompanies him everywhere. Let him think of

God as often as he can, especially when he is in the greatest danger. Just a little lifting up of the heart is enough. A little remembrance of God, one act of inner worship, even though it is during a march with sword in hand, is sufficient. Such prayers, however brief, are very acceptable to God. Far from diminishing a soldier's courage in times of danger, they actually serve to fortify it.

Let him think of God as often as he can. Let him gradually develop within himself this small but sacred practice. Nobody notices it, and nothing is easier than to repeat these little internal adorations often during the day. Recommend to him, if you please, that he be mindful of God as often as he can in the manner I have mentioned. It is appropriate and necessary for a soldier, who is daily exposed to life-threatening situations and thinking of eternal salvation, to do this. I hope that God will help him and his family, to whom I present my service, being theirs and yours.

FOURTH LETTER

I have taken this opportunity to communicate to you the ideas of a member of our priory concerning the marvelous results and continuous blessings which he receives from the presence of God. [In this letter Brother Lawrence speaks of himself in the third person.] Let us both profit by them.

For the forty years that he has been in this religious order, his continual practice has been to always be with God. He seeks to do nothing, say nothing, and think nothing which may displease Him. He does this purely for the love of God, and because God deserves infinitely more.

He is now so accustomed to that Divine Presence, that he receives from it continual help on all occasions. For about thirty years, his soul has been filled with joy that is so continual, and sometimes so great, that he is forced to use effort to control it in order to prevent it from appearing outwardly.

Sometimes when he becomes aware that he is a little absent from this Divine presence, God immediately makes Himself felt in his soul in order to call him back. This happens most often when he is engaged in some outward activity. When this happens, he responds with perfect faithfulness to these inward impulses. He lifts his heart towards God by a meek and tender surrender to God or by words of love that come naturally upon these occasions. For example, he may say, "My God, I am completely devoted to

You. Lord, remake me according to Your heart." Then it feels to him that the God of love is satisfied with these few words. So he relaxes again and rests in the depth and center of his soul. This experience gives him an assurance that God is always in the depth or bottom of his soul. It makes him incapable of doubting it, no matter what may happen.

What contentment and satisfaction he enjoys! He continually finds within himself a great treasure. He is no longer anxiously searching after it, but it is always open before him, and he may take whatever he pleases from it.

He complains a lot about our blindness. He often cries, saying that we are to be pitied because we are content with so little. He says that God has infinite treasure to bestow, and yet we are satisfied with a little feeling of religious devotion which passes in a moment. We are blind, and we hinder God and stop the current of His grace. But when God finds a soul penetrated with a living faith, He pours into it His grace and blessings plentifully. They flow like a torrent, finding a way around every obstacle, spreading out with extravagant and reckless abundance.

Yes, we often stop this flood because of the little value we place upon it. But let us stop it no more. Let us go inside ourselves and break down the flood barriers which hinder it. Let us make a path for grace. Let us redeem the lost time, for we may have little time left. Death follows us closely, and we should be prepared for it. We die but once, and a mistake made at that time is irreversible.

I repeat, let us go inside ourselves. Time passes quickly, and there is no room for delay. Our souls are at stake. I believe you have done this and that you will not be surprised. I commend you for it. It is the one thing necessary. Nevertheless we must always work at it. In the spiritual life, not to advance is to retreat. Those who have the wind of the Holy Spirit go forward even in sleep. If the ship of our soul is still tossed with winds and storms, let us awake the Lord, who sleeps in it, and He will quickly calm the sea.

I have taken the liberty to impart to you these thoughts, so that you may compare them with your own. They will help to kindle and inflame your spiritual inclinations if they should become cooled, which would be a great misfortune. Let us both remember our early enthusiasm. Let us profit by the example and the ideas of this brother, who is little known in the world, but known by God and intimately caressed by Him.

I will pray for you. Pray also for me. I am yours in our Lord.

FIFTH LETTER

Today I received two books and a letter from a Sister, who is preparing to make her profession of vows. She desires the prayers of your religious order and your community in particular. I perceive that she places high value on your prayers, and therefore I hope you will not disappoint her. Pray to God that she may offer herself as a sacrifice in the light of His love alone, and with a firm commitment to be wholly devoted to Him.

I will send you one of these books, which describes the presence of God. In my opinion, it is a subject which sums up the whole spiritual life. It seems to me that whoever faithfully practices it will soon become spiritual.

To practice this correctly, the heart must be empty of all other things. God will possess the heart alone. He cannot possess it solely without emptying it of everything else. He cannot act in the heart, and do what He wants within it, unless it is empty.

There is no sweeter and delightful life than that of continual communion with God. Only those who experience this and practice it can comprehend it. Yet I do not advise you to undertake this practice from that motive. We should not seek pleasure in this exercise. Instead let us do it out of love and because God desires it.

If I were I a preacher, I would preach the practice of the presence of God above all things. If I were a spiritual director, I would advise everyone to practice it. This is how necessary I think it is, and it is also easy.

Oh! If we realized our need for the grace and assistance of God, we would never lose sight of Him, not even for a moment. Believe me in this matter. Right now make a binding and sacred resolution never to willfully forget Him again. Spend the rest of your life in His sacred presence, even if loving him means to be deprived of all other comforts.

Begin this task with your whole heart. If you do it as you ought, you can be assured that you will soon see results. I will assist you by praying for you, as poor as my prayers are. I commend myself earnestly to you and to those of your holy community.

SIXTH LETTER

I have received from Mrs. [name omitted] the things which you gave her to pass on to me. I wonder why you have not also given me your thoughts about the little book I sent you. You must have received it. I encourage you to begin this practice, even at your advanced age. It is better late than never.

I cannot imagine how religious persons can be satisfied without the practice of the presence of God. Personally, I dwell with Him in the depths of the center of my soul as much as I can. When I am with Him in his manner, I fear nothing. But when I turn from Him, it is unbearable.

This exercise does not tire the body. However it may be helpful sometimes, perhaps often, to abstain from some of the little innocent and lawful bodily pleasures. God will not permit a soul, which desires to be devoted entirely to Him, to also desire other pleasures than Him. This seems more than reasonable.

I am not saying that we should put any intense constraint upon ourselves. No, we must serve God in holy freedom. We must do our activities faithfully, without trouble or anxiety.

We are to bring our mind back to God gently and quietly whenever we find it wandering from Him.

It is, however, necessary to put our whole trust in God, laying aside all other concerns, even some particular forms of devotion. Such devotions, though very good in themselves, can be practiced excessively. They are only a means to attain to an end. When by the exercise of the presence of God we are with Him who is our end, it is unnecessary to return to the means. Instead we should continue in our love for Him, persevering in His holy presence. We can do this through an act of praise, adoration, or yearning. We can do this through an act of surrender, thanksgiving, or any other way that our spirit can invent.

Do not be discouraged by the natural resistance that you might experience in doing this practice. You must be forceful with yourself. In the beginning, one often thinks of this practice as wasting time. But you must continue and persevere in it, even unto death, triumphing over all the difficulties that may occur. I recommend myself to the prayers of your holy community, and you in particular. I am yours in our Lord.

SEVENTH LETTER

I feel very sorry for you. It is extremely important that you give your responsibilities to others, and spend the rest of your life solely in worshiping God. He does not require a lot from us - just a little remembrance of Him once in a while, a little worship, and sometimes to pray for His grace. Offer your troubles to Him and give thanks to Him for the blessings He has given you and continues to give you. In the midst of your troubles, comfort yourself with Him as often as you can. Lift up your heart to Him, even during meals and when you are in the company of others. The littlest remembrance will always be acceptable to Him. You do not need to cry out loud. He is nearer to us than we know.

It is not necessary to be in church to be with God. We can make our heart a chapel where we can withdraw from time to time, and commune with Him in meekness, humility, and love. Everyone is capable of this type of intimate communion with God, some more, some less. God knows what we are able to do. So let us begin to do it. He expects but one heartfelt commitment from us. Have courage. We have little time to live. You are nearly sixty-four, and I am almost eighty. Let us live and die with God.

When we are with Him, even sufferings will be sweet and pleasant to us. Without Him even the greatest pleasures will seem like cruel punishments. Praise God for everything! Amen.

Gradually by degrees, train yourself to worship Him and seek His grace. Offer Him your heart from time to time in the midst of your daily work. Do it every minute of the day, if you can. Do not restrict yourself to certain religious rules or forms of devotion. Instead act with a general trust in God, with love and humility. You can be assured of my poor prayers, and that I am their servant and yours particularly.

EIGHTH LETTER

What you are telling me is nothing new. You are not the only one who has trouble with wandering thoughts. Our minds are extremely unfocussed. But our will is the master of all our faculties, and it is able to rein them in and carry them to God, which is their final goal.

When the mind first undertakes spiritual devotion, it has the bad habits of wandering and distraction. These are difficult to overcome and pull us against our will toward worldly things.

One solution is to confess our faults and humble ourselves before God. I advise you not to use a lot of words in prayer. Many words and long monologues are the causes of wandering minds. Instead, hold yourself in prayer before God like a mute and paralyzed beggar at a rich man's gate. Let it be your purpose only to keep your mind in the presence of the Lord. If it sometimes wanders and withdraws itself from Him, do not worry yourself about it. Worry and anxiety distract the mind rather than focus it. The will must bring the mind back in tranquility. If you persevere in this manner, God will be gracious to you.

One way to focus the mind easily during prayer, and preserve it in peace, is not to let it wander too far at other times during the day. You should keep it strictly in the presence of God. If you are accustomed to think of Him often, you will find it easy to keep your mind calm during the time of prayer, or at least to bring it back from its wanderings.

I have told you already in my former letters about the advantages of this practice of the presence of God. So let us do it seriously and pray for one another.

NINTH LETTER

The enclosed letter is my answer to the one I received from [name omitted]. Please deliver it to her. She seems to be full of good intentions, but she wants to move faster than grace. One does not become holy all at once. I recommend her to you. We ought to help one another by our advice, and even more by our good examples. I hope you will oblige me by letting me know how she is doing from time to time, and whether she remains as fervent and obedient.

Let us remember often that our only purpose in this life is to please God. Everything else is folly and vanity. You and I have lived the monastic life for more than forty years. Have we used those years in loving and serving God, who in His mercy has called us to this state and for that purpose? On the one hand, I am grateful when I reflect upon the great things that God has done for me and continues to do unceasingly. On the other hand, I am filled with shame and confusion when I consider how little use I have made of them, and my little progress in the way of perfection.

By His mercy He has still given us a little more time. Therefore let us begin again in earnest. Let us redeem the lost time. Let us return with full assurance to the Father of mercies, who is always ready to receive us tenderly. Let us renounce completely, for love of Him, everything that is not God. He deserves infinitely more than we give. Let us think of Him perpetually. Let us put all our trust in Him. I have no doubt that we will soon see the results of it. We shall receive the abundance of His grace, through which we can do all things, and without which we can do nothing but sin.

We cannot escape the dangers of life except with the real and continual help of God. Let us ask Him for it constantly. How can we pray to Him without being with Him? How can we be with Him unless we think of Him often? And how can we think of Him often unless we make this a holy habit?

You will probably tell me that I am always saying the same thing. It is true. It is because this is the best and easiest method I know. I use no other, and therefore I advise everyone in the world to do it. We must know God before we can love God. In order to know God, we must think of Him often. When we grow to love Him, then we shall think of Him often. Our heart will be where our treasure is. This is an argument which deserves your consideration.

TENTH LETTER

It has been difficult to bring myself to write to Monsieur [name omitted]. I do it now only because you and Madame want me to. Please add his address and send this on to him.

I am very pleased with the trust that you have in God. I hope that He increases it in you more and more. We cannot have too much trust in such a good and faithful Friend, who will never fail us in this world or the next.

If Monsieur takes advantage of the loss he has suffered, and puts all his confidence in God, then God will give him another friend, more powerful and more inclined to serve him. God works in our hearts according to His will. Perhaps Monsieur was too attached to the one he has lost. We should love our friends, but not so much that it encroaches upon our love of God, which must be primary.

Please remember that I have recommended that you meditate often on God, day and night, during business and recreation. He is always near you and with you; do not leave Him alone. You would consider it rude to ignore a friend who came to visit you. Then why neglect God? Do not forget Him. Meditate on Him often.

Adore Him continually. Live and die with Him. This is the glorious vocation of a Christian. You could say that this is our profession. If we do not know how to do it, then we must learn it. I will try to help you with my prayers. I am yours in our Lord.

ELEVENTH LETTER

I do not pray that you be delivered from pain. But I earnestly pray to God that He will give you strength and patience to bear the pain. Comfort yourself in Him who holds you fastened to the cross. He will free you when He thinks it is the right time. Happy are those who suffer with Him. Accustom yourself to suffer in this manner. Seek strength from Him to endure the pain for as long as He thinks necessary.

Worldly people do not comprehend such truths. That is not surprising since they suffer like what they are, and not like Christians. They consider sickness as a curse of nature and not as a blessing from God. Seeing it only in that light, they find no redeeming value in it - only grief and distress. But those who consider sickness as coming from the hand of God see it as part of His mercy. They see it as the means that He employs for their salvation. Consequently they experience great sweetness and consolation in it.

I wish I could convince you that God is often, in one sense, nearer to us and more effectively present with us in sickness than in health. Rely on no other Physician. According to my understanding, He has the cure. Put all your trust in Him, and you will find that you will recover soon. We often delay healing by putting greater confidence in earthly physicians than in God.

Whatever remedies you take will succeed only insofar as He permits. When pains come from God, only God can cure them. He often sends diseases of the body to cure diseases of the soul. Comfort yourself with the sovereign Physician of both soul and body.

I suspect that you will tell me that I can say these things because I am very comfortable, and that I eat and drink at the table of the Lord. You may have reason to think so. But do you think that a criminal awaiting execution would not feel discomfort if there were no assurance of pardon, even if his last meal were served at the king's table by the king himself? I believe he would feel extreme discomfort, which nothing could lessen except trust in the goodness of his sovereign. So I assure you that whatever pleasures I taste at the table of my King, my sins are always present before my eyes. The uncertainty of my pardon tortures me, though I must admit that even that torture itself is pleasing.

Be satisfied with the condition in which God places you. However happy you may think I am, the truth is that I envy you. Pain and suffering would be a paradise to me if I were suffering with God. The greatest pleasures would be hell for me, if I were to enjoy them without God. My greatest comfort would be to suffer something for His sake.

In a little while I must go to God. What comforts me most in this life is that I now see Him by faith. I see Him so clearly that sometimes I want to say, "I do not believe any longer; I see!" I experience what faith teaches. I will live and die with Him in this assurance and practice of faith.

Continue always with God. It is the only strength and comfort for your suffering. I will pray that He be with you. I am at your service.

TWELFTH LETTER

If we continually practiced the presence of God, physical diseases would be greatly diminished. God permits us to suffer a little in order to purify our souls and help us continue with Him.

Be courageous. Offer your pain continually to God. Pray to Him for the strength to endure. Most importantly, maintain a habit of the awareness of God. Forget Him as seldom as you can. Adore Him in your illness. Offer yourself to Him repeatedly. When you are in the midst of suffering, beseech Him humbly and affectionately, as a child would implore his father, to conform you to His holy will. I shall try to assist you with my poor prayers.

God has many ways of drawing us to Himself. Sometimes He hides Himself from us. Only faith will not fail us in time of need. Complete confidence in God should be our strength and foundation.

I do not know how God will deal with me. I am always happy. Everyone else suffers. Even though I deserve the severest discipline, I feel joy so continuously and so abundantly that I can hardly contain it.

I would gladly ask God if I could share your sufferings, but I know my weakness is great. If He left me alone for one moment, I would be the most wretched person alive. Yet I do not know how He could possibly leave me alone. Faith gives me a strong conviction, stronger than my senses ever could, that He never forsakes us, unless we first forsake Him. Let us fear to leave Him. Let us be always with Him. Let us live and die in His presence. Pray for me, and I will pray for you.

THIRTEENTH LETTER

It pains me to see you suffer for so long. It gives me some consolation, and it may sweeten your grief, to know that this is proof of God's love for you. View your suffering in this manner, and you will be able to bear it more easily. It is my opinion that you should forget the human remedies now and resign yourself fully to the providence of God. Perhaps He is only waiting for that perfect resignation and trust in order to cure you. In spite of all the medical care you have received, the physicians have not been successful in curing you, and your illness is only getting worse. Therefore it would not be testing God to abandon yourself into His hands, and expect everything from Him.

I told you in my last letter that God sometimes permits bodily diseases in order to cure problems of the soul. Have courage then.

Make a virtue of necessity. Don't ask God for deliverance from your pain, but for strength to bear it resolutely. Bear it for the love of Him, as much as He wills, for as long as He wills it.

Such prayers are against our nature, yet they are most acceptable to God, and sweet to those who love Him. Love sweetens pain. When one loves God, one suffers for His sake with joy and courage. I urge you to comfort yourself with Him, who is the only Physician able to cure all our maladies. He is the Father of the afflicted, and He is always available to help us. He loves us infinitely more than we can imagine. Love Him in return, and do not seek consolation elsewhere. I hope you will soon receive it. Adieu. I will be praying for you, as poor as my prayers are. I shall be always yours in our Lord.

FOURTEENTH LETTER

I thank our Lord that you have received some relief from your suffering, for I know that this was what you have been wanting. I have been near death often. I have never been as content as I was then. Therefore I did not pray for relief, but I prayed for strength to suffer with courage, humility, and love. How sweet is it to suffer with God! However great the suffering may be, we receive it with love. It is paradise to suffer and be with Him.

If we desire to enjoy the peace of paradise in this life, we must accustom ourselves to intimate, humble, loving communion with Him. We must keep our spirits from wandering away from Him on any occasion. We must make our heart a spiritual temple where we can adore Him continually. We must watch incessantly over ourselves, so that we may not do, say, nor think anything that may offend Him. When our minds are focused on God, suffering will be filled with peace and solace.

In the beginning it is very difficult to arrive at this state, for we must act purely in faith. Even though it is difficult, we also know that we can do all things with the grace of God, which He never refuses to give to those who ask for it earnestly. Knock, and persevere in knocking. I assure you that He will open to you in His time, and immediately grant you what He has delayed giving you during these many years. Adieu. Pray for me, as I pray for you. I hope to see Him soon.

FIFTEENTH LETTER

God knows best what we need, and everything that He does is for our good. If we realized how much He loves us, we would always be willing to receive both the sweet and the bitter equally and indifferently from His hand. Everything that came from Him would please us. The most painful afflictions appear intolerable only when we view them in the wrong light. When we understand that it is the hand of God that dispenses them, and we know that it is our loving Father who humbles and wounds us, then our sufferings lose their bitterness. They even become sources of consolation.

May all our energy be devoted to knowing God. The more one knows Him, the more one desires to know Him. Knowledge is commonly understood as the measure of love. The deeper and more extensive our knowledge is, the greater will be our love. If our love of God is great, we will love Him equally in pain and pleasure.

Let us not amuse ourselves by seeking God or loving God in order to receive blessings from God, no matter how lofty those blessings may be. Such blessings, however great, cannot bring us as near to God as one simple movement of faith. Let us seek Him by faith often. He is within us; do not seek Him elsewhere. Are we not rude and blameworthy, if we leave Him alone and busy ourselves with trifles, which do not please Him and may even offend Him? These trifles will one day cost us dearly.

Let us be devoted to Him earnestly. Let us cast away everything else from our hearts. He desires to possess them exclusively. Beg this favor from Him. If we do our part, we shall soon see the transformation within us that we desire. I cannot thank Him enough for the comfort He has given you. I hope by his grace to see Him in a few days. Let us pray for one another.

[Lawrence took to his bed two days after he wrote this letter and died within the week.]

SPIRITUAL MAXIMS

MEANS FOR ATTAINING TO THE PRESENCE OF GOD

1. We are to practice honoring God and His Glory in everything that we do and say. This is our goal: to offer to God a sacrifice of perfect worship in this life and throughout eternity. We should firmly resolve to overcome every difficulty that we encounter in reaching this goal by the grace of God.

2. When we begin the spiritual life, we should do a thorough inquiry into our human nature, probing to its deepest depths. We will find that we are unworthy of the name of Christ. We are subject to all sorts of difficulties and weaknesses. These trouble us and damage our spiritual health. They cause us to waver and be unstable in our emotions and attitudes. We are creatures chastened and humbled by God through countless sufferings and adversities, inside and outside.

3. We must steadfastly believe, and never doubt, that all suffering is for our good. God is

disciplining us. His Divine Providence permits our souls to pass through many difficult experiences and times of trial. We are to endure various sorrows and sufferings for the love of God, for as long as He deems it necessary. Without submission of the heart and spirit to the will of God, devotion and perfection cannot exist.

4. The higher the spiritual state to which a soul aspires, the more it is dependent on grace. The grace of God is necessary every moment, for without it the soul can do nothing. The world, the flesh, and the devil join forces and assault the soul directly and relentlessly. Without humble reliance on the ever-present assistance of God, they drag the soul down in spite of all resistance. To rely on God's help seems difficult, but grace makes it easy, and it brings joy.

NECESSARY PRACTICES FOR ATTAINING TO THE SPIRITUAL LIFE

1. The practice of the Presence of God is the most holy, the most all-encompassing, and the most necessary practice of the spiritual life. It trains the soul to find its joy in His Divine Companionship. At all times and at every moment, it engages the soul in humble and loving communion with Him, without rules or

methods. This is practiced in all circumstances, in times of temptation and tribulation, spiritual dryness and apathy, and even when we fall into unfaithfulness and sin.

2. We should commit ourselves unceasingly to this one goal: that everything we do be little acts of communion with God. This must be natural and not artificial, coming from the purity and simplicity of the heart.

3. We must do everything thoughtfully and mindfully, without impulsiveness or rashness, which indicate an undisciplined mind. We must go about our daily activities quietly, calmly, and lovingly, asking Him to bless the work of our hands. By keeping our heart and mind fixed on God, we shall bruise the head of the evil one, and cast his weapons to the ground.

4. When we are busy meditating on spiritual things, or doing our daily devotions, or even raising our voice in prayer, we ought to stop every once in a while to worship God in the depth of our being. Taste Him as if in passing. Touch Him, as it were, by stealth. Know that God is with you in everything you do. He is at the very depth and center of your soul. Why not pause for a moment from time to time in the midst of your busyness, even during the act of prayer, to worship Him within your soul? Why

not praise Him, ask for His help, offer Him the service of your heart, and give Him thanks for all His loving-kindnesses and tender mercies?

What offering is more acceptable to God than to, periodically throughout the day, leave behind the things of our outward senses and withdraw within to worship Him in the secret place of the soul? By doing this we destroy the love of self, which can survive only among the things of sense. These times of quiet retirement with God rid us unconsciously of self-love.

Truly we could give God no greater evidence of our trust and faithfulness than by turning from the creation to find our joy in the present moment in the Creator. I am not suggesting that we completely disregard forever the outward things that are around us. That is impossible. Prudence, the mother of the virtues, must be your guide. Yet it is a common error of religious persons to neglect this practice of stopping for a moment in order to worship God in the depth of their soul and enjoy briefly the peace of communion with Him. I am digressing here, but it seemed necessary. Let us return to our subject.

5. Our acts of worship are to be prompted and guided by faith. We must honestly believe that God is really within our souls. We must believe that we should worship Him, love Him, and

serve Him in spirit and in truth. We must believe that He sees all and that all hearts are open to Him, both our own and those of all His creatures. We must believe that He is self-existent and that all His creatures live and move and have their being in him. We believe that His Perfection is infinite and sovereign, and demands the full surrender of our whole selves, body and soul. It is only right that we owe Him all our thoughts, words and actions. Let us pay our debt.

6. It is necessary to examine ourselves carefully to find out which virtues we lack most, and which are the hardest for us to acquire. We should seek to discover which sins most easily ensnare us, and at what times and on what occasions we usually fall. In time of struggle we ought to turn to God with perfect confidence, abiding steadfastly in the Presence of His Divine Majesty. In lowly adoration we can tell Him our sorrows and our failures, asking Him lovingly for the assistance of His grace. In our weakness we shall find strength in Him.

IT IS REQUIRED OF US TO WORSHIP GOD IN SPIRIT AND IN TRUTH

There are three points which must be addressed concerning this matter:

1. To worship God in spirit and in truth means to offer to Him the worship that we owe. God is a Spirit; therefore we must worship Him in spirit and in truth. This means to present to Him true and humble spiritual worship in the very depth of our being. Only God can see this worship. If this is offered unceasingly, it will eventually become natural for us. It will be as if He were one with our soul, and our soul one with Him. Practice will make this clear.

2. To worship God in truth is to acknowledge Him to be what He is, and to acknowledge ourselves to be what we are. To worship Him in truth is to acknowledge with heartfelt sincerity what God truly is: infinitely perfect, worthy of infinite adoration, infinitely removed from sin, and so on, for all the Divine attributes. The man who does not employ all his powers to render to this great God the worship that is due Him is not being guided by reason.

3. Furthermore, to worship God in truth is to confess that we live our lives entirely contrary to His will. We know that if we were willing, He would make us conformable to Him. Who will be guilty of such folly as to withhold, even for a moment, the reverence love, service and unceasing worship that we owe Him?

THE UNION OF THE SOUL WITH GOD

There are three degrees of union of the soul with God. The first degree is general union, the second is momentary union, and the third is authentic union.

1. General union is when one realizes that the soul is always united to God solely by grace.

2. Momentary union (which is experiential, but not actual) is when we experience union with God through performing a certain action. We remain united to Him only for as long as we are performing that action.

3. Authentic union is perfect union. In the other types the soul is passive, almost as if it were sleeping. In genuine union the soul is intensely active. Its movements are quicker than fire, more luminous than the sun unobscured by any passing cloud. We can be deceived by our feelings in regard to this union. It is not a fleeting emotion, which would prompt us to cry "My God, I love You with all my heart!" Instead it is a state of soul. I cannot find the words to describe it, but I will try. It is deeply spiritual, yet very simple. It fills us with a joy that is completely calm, and with a love that is very humble and reverent. It lifts the soul aloft to

heights where the reality of God's love compels the soul to adore Him. The soul embraces Him with a tenderness that cannot be expressed. It must be experienced to be understood.

4. All who aspire to union with the Divine should be careful concerning the will. Whatever is exciting pleases the will; that is the way the will works. Remember that God is beyond our understanding. To be united to God it is necessary to deny the will all tastes and pleasures, both physical and spiritual. When detached in this manner, it is free to love God above all things. If the will can know God at all, it can do so only through love. There is a great difference between the preferences and feelings of the will and its work. The will's preferences and feelings are bound up in the human soul, while its work, which is love, finds its only purpose in God.

THE PRESENCE OF GOD

1. The Presence of God is our spirit in contact with God. It is a realization that God is present, made known to us either by the imagination or the understanding.

2. I have a friend who has been practicing the realization of the Presence of God through

understanding for forty years. He gives it many names. Sometimes he calls it a Simple Act, or a clear and distinct knowledge of God. At other times he refers to it as seeing through a glass, a loving gaze, or an inward sense of God. He also calls it waiting on God, a silent conversation with Him, a rest in Him, or the life and peace of the Soul. My friend tells me that all these ways of expressing the sense of the Presence of God comes to the same thing: Presence fills his soul very naturally.

3. He says that by unceasing effort, by continually bringing his mind back to the Presence of God, a habit has formed within him. As soon as he is finished with his daily work, and even while he is doing his work, his soul lifts itself up above all earthly concerns, without any effort or thought by him. It dwells firmly fixed on God as its center and place of rest. Faith is almost always his companion at such times. Then his soul's joy is complete. This is what he calls Actual Presence, and includes all other types and much more. At such times he feels that there is only God and him in the world. He holds unbroken communion with God, asking Him to supply all his needs, and finding fullness of joy in His Presence.

4. Let us understand well that this fellowship with God happens in the depth of one's being. It

is there that the soul speaks to God, heart to heart. A great and profound peace comes over the soul during this communion. Everything that is happening on the outside does not concern the soul. The outside world is like a brush fire, flaring up briefly and quickly burning itself out. Rarely do the cares of this world intrude to disrupt the peace that is within.

5. Coming back to our consideration of the Presence of God, you must know that the tender and loving light of God's countenance kindles a divine fire of love for God within the soul that ardently embraces it. This fire is so great that one is compelled to control the outward expression of feelings.

6. We would be very surprised if we knew what conversation the soul has with God at these times. God seems to delight in this communion with our soul to such an extent that He bestows innumerable blessings, in order to ensure that the soul will abide with Him forever. It is almost as if He feared that the soul would turn away from Him again to things of earth. Therefore He provides for it lavishly. The soul finds divine nourishment in faith beyond its highest thought and desire; this is a boundless joy. All this takes place without any effort from the soul beyond simple consent.

7. The Presence of God is the life and nourishment of the soul. With the aid of His grace, it can attain this Presence through the conscientious exercise of the practices which I will now put forth.

PRACTICES FOR REALIZING THE PRESENCE OF GOD

1. The first practice is purity of life. We are to guard ourselves carefully, lest we do or say or think anything which might be displeasing to God. When any such thing happens, then it is important to repent of it immediately, humbly asking His forgiveness.

2. The second is faithfulness in the practice of His Presence. We are to keep the soul's gaze fixed on God in faith - calmly, humbly, and lovingly, without allowing the appearance of anxious thoughts and emotions.

3. Make it your practice, before beginning any task, to look to God, even if it is just for a moment. Look to God while you doing any activity and also after you have completed it. It takes much time and patience to perfect this practice, so do not be discouraged by failure. This habit is only developed with much

difficulty. Yet when it is achieved, how great will be your joy!

The heart is the first thing in us to have life, and it has power over the body. Is it not right that the heart should also be the first and last to love and worship God when we begin and end any task? This is true whether the task is spiritual or physical. It is true in all the normal activities of life. Therefore it is in the heart, that we ought to strive to make a habit of gazing on God. But it is important to bring the heart to this obedience, as I have already said, quite simply, without strain or effort.

4. Let me suggest some simple words that those who begin this practice can use privately. Use prayers such as: "My God, I am wholly Yours. O God of Love, I love You with all my heart. Lord, make my heart even as Yours." Use other similar words, as love moves you at the moment. But be careful that your mind does not wander back to the world again. Keep it fixed on God alone, so that, being subdued by the will, it may be trained to abide with God.

5. This practice of the Presence of God is somewhat difficult at the beginning. Yet if it is pursued faithfully, it works imperceptibly within the soul to produce marvelous results. It draws down God's grace abundantly, and leads

the soul gradually to the ever-present vision of God as loving and beloved. It is the most spiritual, the most real, the most free, and most life-giving form of prayer.

6. Remember that to attain to this state, we must deny the senses. No soul, which takes delight in worldly things, can find full joy in the Presence of God. To be with Him we must leave behind the creature.

THE BENEFITS OF THE PRESENCE OF GOD

1. The first benefit which the soul receives from the Presence of God is that faith grows more alive and active in all circumstances of life. This is particularly true when we feel in need. It obtains for us the assistance of His grace in times of temptation and trial. This practice accustoms us to take faith as our guide. By the simple remembrance of God, the soul sees and feels that God is present. It calls upon Him freely with the assurance of response, and it receives everything it needs. By faith the soul draws very close to the Blessed State. The higher it advances, the more lively faith grows. Finally the eye of faith becomes so clear that the soul can almost say, "Faith is swallowed up in Sight, I see and I experience!"

2. The practice of the Presence of God strengthens us in Hope. Our hope grows in proportion to our knowledge. This holy practice penetrates into the hidden mysteries of God In proportion to our faith. To the same degree it discovers in Him beauty beyond imagining, infinitely surpassing that of earth, equal to that of the most holy souls and angels. Our hope grows ever stronger, sustained and invigorated by the fullness of the bliss to which it aspires to and which it already partially tastes.

3. Hope breathes into the will a distrust of visible things, and sets it aflame with the consuming fire of Divine love. For God's love is truly a consuming fire, burning to ashes all that is contrary to His will. The soul that is kindled cannot live except in the Presence of God. This Presence produces within the heart a consecrated zeal, a holy ardor, and a violent passion to see this God known and loved, served and worshipped, by all His creatures.

4. By the practice of the Presence of God, by steadfastly gazing upon Him, the soul comes to a full and deep knowledge of God. It has Unclouded Vision. Its life is spent in unceasing acts of love and worship, contrition and simple trust, praise, prayer, and service. At times life seems to be one long unbroken practice of His Divine Presence. I know that there are not many

who reach this state. It is a grace which God bestows only on very few chosen souls.

Books by Marshall Davis

Thank God for Atheists: What Christians Can Learn
from the New Atheism

Experiencing God Directly: The Way of Christian
Nonduality

The Tao of Christ: A Christian Version of the Tao Te
Ching

Living Presence: A Guide to Everyday Awareness of
God

More Than a Purpose: An Evangelical Response to
Rick Warren and the Megachurch Movement

The Baptist Church Covenant: Its History and Meaning

A People Called Baptist: An Introduction to Baptist
History & Heritage

The Practice of the Presence of God in Modern
English by Brother Lawrence, translated by Marshall
Davis

The Gospel of Christ in the Song of Songs

Esther

The Hidden Ones